Math Matters!

Chance
and
Average

Look out for these sections to help
you learn more about each topic:

Remember...
This provides a summary of the key
concept(s) on each two-page entry.
Use it to revise what you have
learned.

Word check
These are new and important words
that help you understand the ideas
presented on each two-page entry.

All of the word check entries in
this book are shown in the glossary
on page 45. The versions in the
glossary are sometimes more
extensive explanations.

Book link...
Although this book can be used on
its own, other titles in the *Math
Matters!* set may provide more
information on certain topics. This
section tells you which other titles to
refer to.

Series concept by *Brian Knapp and Duncan McCrae*
Text contributed by *Brian Knapp and Colin Bass*
Design and production by *Duncan McCrae*
Illustrations of characters by *Nicolas Debon*
Digital illustrations by *David Woodroffe*
Other illustrations by *Peter Bull Art Studio*
Editing by *Lorna Gilbert and Barbara Carragher*
Layout by *Duncan McCrae and Mark Palmer*
Reprographics by *Global Colour*
Printed and bound by *LEGO SpA, Italy*

**First Published in the United States in 1999
by Grolier Educational, Sherman Turnpike,
Danbury, CT 06816**

Copyright © 1999
Atlantic Europe Publishing Company Limited

Reprinted 2001

Library of Congress Cataloging-in-Publication Data
Math Matters!
p. cm.
Includes indexes.
Contents: v.1.Numbers — v.2.Adding — v.3.Subtracting —
v.4.Multiplying — v.5.Dividing — v.6.Decimals — v.7.Fractions –
v.8.Shape — v.9.Size — v.10.Tables and Charts — v.11.Grids and
Graphs — v.12.Chance and Average — v.13.Mental Arithmetic
ISBN 0–7172–9294–0 (set: alk. paper). — ISBN 0–7172–9295–9 (v.1:
alk. paper). — ISBN 0–7172–9296–7 (v.2: alk. paper). — ISBN 0–7172–
9297–5 (v.3: alk. paper). — ISBN 0–7172–9298–3 (v.4: alk. paper). —
ISBN 0–7172–9299–1 (v.5: alk. paper). — ISBN 0–7172–9300–9 (v.6:
alk. paper). — ISBN 0–7172–9301–7 (v.7: alk. paper). — ISBN 0–7172–
9302–5 (v.8: alk. paper). — ISBN 0–7172–9303–3 (v.9: alk. paper). —
ISBN 0–7172–9304–1 (v.10: alk. paper). — ISBN 0–7172–9305–X
(v.11: alk. paper). — ISBN 0–7172–9306–8 (v.12: alk. paper). — ISBN
0–7172–9307–6 (v.13: alk. paper).

1. Mathematics — Juvenile literature. [1. Mathematics.]
I. Grolier Educational Corporation.
QA40.5.M38   1998
510 — dc21   98–7404
                                                                  CIP
                                                                   AC

This book is manufactured from sustainable managed forests.
For every tree cut down at least one more is planted.

Contents

Introduction

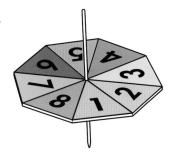

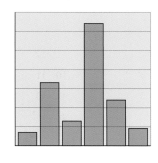

$\dfrac{3}{4}$

75%

0.75

3 in 4

"Well, I'm not certain if that is true…" This is a common saying that leads us on the road to thinking about how sure or unsure we might be. Other words about certainty are likely and probable.

In fact, much of the mathematics of finding out about how likely something is to happen dates back to 1654.

The Chevalier de Méré, who was a professional gambler, was having bad luck. He had been playing a game in which he thought that he had a good chance of winning, but he was steadily losing money. He mentioned it to his mathematician friend, Blaise Pascal. Pascal began to work out rules that

$\dfrac{63.8}{5} = 12.76$

	1	2	3	4	5	6
6	7	8	9	10	11	12
5	6	7	8	9	10	11
4	5	6	7	8	9	10
3	4	5	6	7	8	9
2	3	4	5	6	7	8
1	2	3	4	5	6	7

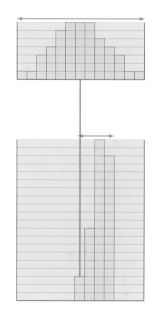

other people could use to find out for themselves how likely a thing was to happen. These rules led to the part of mathematics known as statistics.

All of the methods shown in this book started with Pascal. Today the rules are still widely used, as you will see. This is because many people want to know about the likelihood of a certain thing happening. For example, weather forecasters tell us about the likelihood of storms each day by saying, "there is a **70%** chance of a shower, or a **40%** chance of snow," and so on.

Find out about chance and what we can do with it in this book.

$$\frac{4}{52}$$

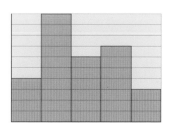

The meaning of chance

Chance is all about the likelihood that something will happen. One of the most everyday situations you will find this is in the daily weather forecast.

Will it rain?

Do you think it will rain today? In some places in the world the weather is very predictable, even without weather forecasts. A Bedouin in the Sahara Desert of North Africa, for example, is unlikely to ask his friend if it will rain, because it hardly ever rains, and when it does, heavy clouds beforehand make the coming downpour obvious.

▼ **Words used to describe chance**

Chances out of 10	Chance, written as a percent	Meaning
$\frac{10}{10}$	100%	Absolutely certain
$\frac{9}{10}$	90%	Highly likely
$\frac{8}{10}$	80%	
$\frac{7}{10}$	70%	Quite likely
$\frac{6}{10}$	60%	
$\frac{5}{10}$	50%	Might or might not
$\frac{4}{10}$	40%	
$\frac{3}{10}$	30%	Not very likely, but don't say we didn't warn you
$\frac{2}{10}$	20%	
$\frac{1}{10}$	10%	Not much chance
$\frac{0}{10}$	0%	Absolutely no chance

In tropical rain forests it rains every afternoon except in the regular rainy season, when it rains all the time.

On the other hand, in many other parts of the world people talk endlessly about the weather because it is very hard to predict. Long dry spells and long wet spells are mixed up with showery periods and sudden surprises.

A weather forecaster can use computers to predict what the weather will be for a day or two ahead. Nevertheless, because we don't know for certain what will happen tomorrow, we can only make a prediction based on what happened in the past.

By studying the past patterns of weather and using scientific equations, the enormous amounts of data that are received by weather stations each day can be used to suggest the forecast for the next few days. But because the weather varies unpredictably, forecasters can still only suggest what they think the chances are of their weather forecast being correct. It is for this reason that they say, for example, there is a **40%** chance of a thundershower today.

Remember... We often use "chance" words in day-to-day talk. These kinds of words are often more accurate than numbers unless we are sure that we have the mathematics to back our numbers up. For example, don't say you are **90%** certain when all you really know is that something is very likely to happen.

Word check:
% : The symbol for percent.
Chance: Something that occurs in an unpredictable way. You can forecast your chances in the long term, but you can never guarantee what will happen next.
Fraction: A special form of division using a numerator and denominator. The line between the two is called a dividing line.
Percent: A number followed by the % symbol means the number is divided by 100. It is a way of writing a fraction.

Even

Some things in this life will <u>never</u> happen. They are <u>impossible</u>. For example, you will not win the lottery if you never buy a ticket for it. Other things <u>almost</u> <u>never</u> happen, although they are <u>possible</u>. For example, you might win a major prize in the lottery if you do buy a ticket. But most people never win. On the other hand, there are some times when you stand an <u>even</u> <u>chance</u> of winning. The following examples show what this means.

Card choosing

Some things are <u>quite</u> <u>likely</u> to happen. For example, a pack of playing cards has **52** cards, of which **26** have red patterns and **26** have black patterns. If you chose one card from this pack, you would not be surprised if it was red.

If you replaced the card and repeated the experiment many times, you would expect about the same number of black cards as red cards. You expect this to happen because you think that in this game, black and red are <u>equally</u> <u>likely</u>. Chance situations like this are often called <u>even</u>.

If, after a long while, the numbers of red and black cards you chose were not roughly equal, you would suspect that there was something <u>unfair</u> going on. Perhaps someone had cheated by removing some black cards from the pack and replacing them with the same number of red ones.

In a <u>fair</u> pack **40** of the cards are numbered, and **12** have pictures. You might describe choosing a numbered card as <u>probable</u>, or <u>quite likely</u>.

Choosing a picture card would be <u>improbable</u>, or <u>unlikely</u>. You would be <u>certain</u> to choose either a red card or a black one.

Coin tossing

This is a clear and simple case of <u>even</u>, or **50:50**, when you get a head or a tail **50%** of the time. Find out more on page 20.

Make sure... Look at the words underlined on these pages to see where they would fit into the table on the previous page.

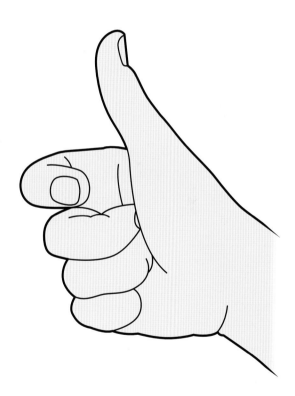

Remember... Even, or **50:50**, is the halfway mark, separating things more likely to happen from those that are less likely to happen.

Work Check
Even: An equal chance of achieving one of the two possible results, such as in coin tossing.

It's equally likely

Here's a simple idea about chance. Even before we can measure how likely things are, we can sometimes tell if they are equally likely. For example, if you toss a coin onto the floor, it is equally likely to land one way up as the other.

If you roll a die (plural dice), each face is as likely to end uppermost as the others. You have six <u>equally likely results</u> called 1, 2, 3, 4, 5, 6.

If you choose one card from a pack of **52** playing cards without looking, then each of the cards is equally likely to be chosen. Which means you have **52** <u>equally likely results</u>.

If you use raffle tickets and there are **1,000** tickets given out, then there are **1,000** equally likely chances of winning if the tickets are chosen without looking.

An equal-chance top

You can make a top that will produce as many equal chances as you wish. For example, if you divide it into 4 equal sectors, you will get four equally likely results whenever you spin the top.

However many equal sectors you draw gives you that many equal chances. So you could divide it into 8, 10, 16, or more sectors.

You can number the sectors 1, 2, 3, 4, 5, 6, 7, 8 (or however many you have). Spin your top on a flat table.

When the top stops, one of the sectors will be touching the table, and that is your result this time. You can spin your top as many times as you like.

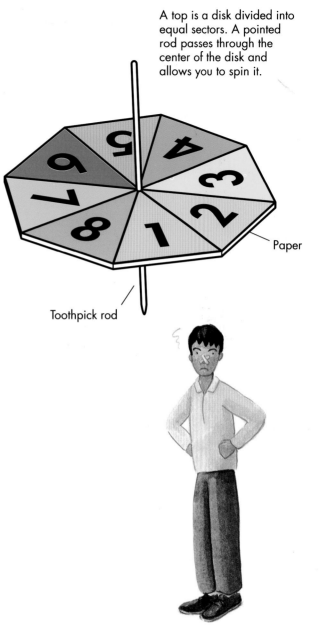

A top is a disk divided into equal sectors. A pointed rod passes through the center of the disk and allows you to spin it.

Paper

Toothpick rod

Book link... To find out more about how to divide a circle into equal pieces, you may need to know about pie charts. Find this in the book *Tables and Charts* in the *Math Matters!* set.

Remember... If you close your eyes and stick a pin in a page of a newspaper to choose a letter of the alphabet, the 26 letters are <u>not</u> equally likely to be picked. That's because words do not use all of the letters of the alphabet equally often. There are more a's than z's on this page, for example.

Word check

Equally likely: Results are called equally likely when there is no reason to think any one of them will occur more often than the others. In an experiment they still might not occur the same number of times. That's chance!

Raffle: A fund-raising lottery with goods as prizes.

Sector: A piece of a circle, like a piece of a pie.

What are my chances?

It is easy to see that if we have **52** cards in a pack, the chances of picking out any one of them, say an ace of spades, from a pack that is face down is **1** in **52**. But what happens if we change the choice? For example, we want to know how likely it is that we will pick a king.

There are four kings in a pack of cards (clubs, diamonds, hearts, spades), so the chance of picking a king is **4** in **52**, which as a fraction is

$$\frac{4}{52}$$

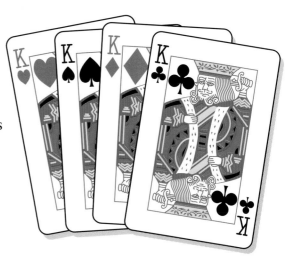

This is a four times better chance than picking the ace of spades or the king of hearts because there is only one of either of those cards in a pack.

The fraction

$$\frac{4}{52}$$

can be simplified to 1/13.

$$\frac{1}{13}$$

So there is **1** chance in **13** of picking a king.

We can make a rule to help us decide on the chances of success. It is the same fraction as that used above, but made into a more general form.

The chance of a success is:

$$\frac{\textbf{number of choices}}{\textbf{total number of options}}$$

To show how easy it is to use, here are some more examples that we used before.

When we roll a die and have to score a "six" to start a board game, the number of options is **6** because any number **1** to **6** can land uppermost.

The chances of success in getting a **6** are:

$$\frac{\textbf{number of ways of scoring a "six" (1)}}{\textbf{total number of equally likely options (6)}}$$

$$= \frac{1}{6}$$

The chances of choosing a "diamond" from a pack of playing cards is:

$$\frac{\textbf{number of "diamonds" in the pack (13)}}{\textbf{number of cards in the pack (52)}}$$

$$= \frac{13}{52}$$

$$= \frac{1}{4}$$

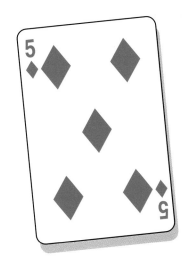

Remember… This only works when the options are equally likely.

Word check

Choices: The things we actually pick from what is available.

Options: The set of equally likely things we can pick from.

How to talk about success

Using numbers to measure chance is the key to understanding how successful you will be.

There are many ways we can write down our chances. We can use fractions, decimals, ratios, or percentages. These are all shown together on the diagram on this page.

Fraction	$\frac{0}{0}$	$\frac{1}{2}$	$\frac{1}{1}$
Percentage	0%	50%	100%
Decimal	0.0	0.5	1.0
Ratio		1 in 2	1 in 1

If you could be successful every time, your chances of success would be expressed by the fraction $\frac{1}{1}$, the decimal 1.0, the percentage 100%, or a ratio of 1 in 1. We would say that we were certain to be successful.

Failure every time, or no success at all, would be the lowest kind of success. This would be the fraction $\frac{0}{0}$, the decimal 0.0, or the percentage 0%. We would say that we would never be successful.

Of course, we are mostly interested in things that fall between these two extremes. Even, when something is expected to happen one in two times, is shown by the fraction $\frac{1}{2}$, the decimal 0.5, the percentage 50%, or the ratio 1 in 2, as you can see in the diagram.

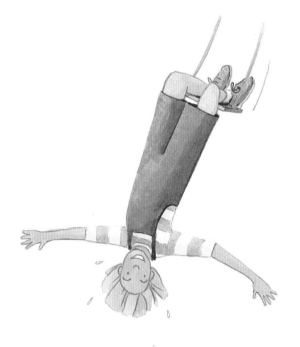

Some examples of chance

Fraction	Percentage	Decimal	Ratio	Description
$\frac{0}{0}$	0%	0.0		never
$\frac{1}{5}$	20%	0.2	1 in 5	not very likely
$\frac{1}{2}$	50%	0.5	1 in 2	even (equally likely)
$\frac{3}{4}$	75%	0.75	3 in 4	quite probable
$\frac{19}{20}$	95%	0.95	19 in 20	very likely
$\frac{1}{1}$	100%	1.0	1 in 1	certain

Book link... Find more about ratios and how to change between fractions, decimals, and percentages in the books *Dividing*, *Fractions*, and *Decimals* in the *Math Matters!* set.

Remember... Chance can be shown as a fraction, a decimal, a percentage, or a ratio.

Word check

Decimal number: A number that contains parts of units as well as whole units. The decimal point is used to separate the units from the parts of a unit.

Ratio: A method of comparing different numbers by placing them on either side of a colon (:); for example 1:2. The numbers must be measured in the same units. The order of the numbers matters. A ratio is like a fraction.

Chance with one or two dice

Lots of board games are played with dice. Here are some of the chances of various numbers coming up.

One die

When only one die is used, it is equally likely that each of the faces will be uppermost when the die stops rolling.

Since there are 6 sides to a die, the chances of any one number coming up is 1 in 6, or ⅙, as we saw on page 13.

But what are the chances of one of a group of numbers coming up using just one die? For example, how likely is it that a 2 or a 3 will roll face up during one throw?

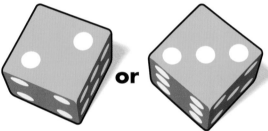

or

In this case we have chosen 2 numbers, and there are a total of 6 options. The chance of a 2 or a 3 rolling face up in one throw can be worked out as follows:

$$\frac{\textbf{numbers of choices}}{\textbf{total number of options}} = \frac{2}{6} = \frac{1}{3}$$

or **1 in 3**

This means that we can expect a 2 or a 3 to fall face up once every three rolls of the die if we roll the die very many times.

Two dice

When two dice are used, the chances of getting a chosen number can more easily be read from a table.

The table on the right shows all the totals you can get from a combination of two dice. They range from 1 + 1 = 2 to 6 + 6 = 12.

You can also see that there are 6 × 6 = 36 possible results.

Suppose we want to know the chances of throwing a total of 9. One answer would be when we throw a blue 4 and a red 5 or a red 4 and a blue 5. Another one would be a blue 6 and a red 3 or a red 6 and a blue 3.

The options that total 9 are shown on the right and have been highlighted in pink on the table.

So the chance of scoring a 9 is 4 out of 36:

$$\frac{4}{36} = \frac{1}{9} \quad \text{or} \quad \textbf{1 in 9}$$

The table also shows how to work out the chances of scoring a double (both dice come up with the same number). Check it out for yourself. There are 6 doubles out of 36 possible results. So the answer is 1 in 6.

	1	2	3	4	5	6
6	7	8	9	10	11	12
5	6	7	8	9	10	11
4	5	6	7	8	9	10
3	4	5	6	7	8	9
2	3	4	5	6	7	8
1	2	3	4	5	6	7

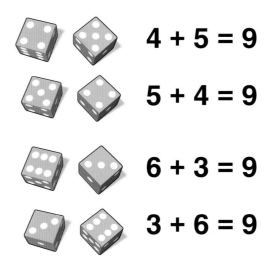

4 + 5 = 9

5 + 4 = 9

6 + 3 = 9

3 + 6 = 9

Remember... 4 + 6 = 10 and 6 + 4 = 10 occur with dice in different ways. The probability of a total score of 10 is $\frac{3}{36} = \frac{1}{12}$.

Raffles

A raffle is a game of chance done for a good cause. But how do you work out your chances of winning? It is really quite simple, as this example shows.

Tom's school raffle

Tom was looking at the raffle prizes at the fair when someone asked him to buy a ticket. There were twelve prizes altogether, and Tom really hoped he could win the football. There were **300** tickets to be sold. Tom worked out the chance of winning the football as a first prize using the fraction on page 12.

$$\frac{\textbf{number of tickets he bought}}{\textbf{total number of tickets sold}}$$

$$= \frac{1}{300}$$

If he bought one ticket, he was very unlikely to win first prize because, as you can see, he only had a **1**-in-**300** chance.

There were three books of tickets: green, blue, and red. All the tickets in each book had different numbers. To increase his chances of winning first prize to **3** in **300** (which is **1%**), Tom decided to buy 1 ticket from the red book, 1 from the green book, and 1 from the blue book.

At the end of the fair one ticket was drawn from the bag without looking. "Red **21**," the head teacher called. Tom looked excitedly through the tickets in his hand. Yes! He had a red ticket numbered **21**. He went to the front, and they let him choose the football.

In fact...

Tom's chances of winning some sort of prize were really better than **1%** (winning first prize). If he had not won first prize, he might have won second prize. The chances of that would be

$$\frac{\textbf{3 tickets still in his hand}}{\textbf{299 tickets still in the bag}}$$

which is still about **1%**. If the winner of the first prize had chosen something else, Tom could still win the football.

Or, he might win it at the third attempt, and so on, until all the prizes had been used.

Remember... Your chances of winning some kind of prize in a raffle are higher than your chance of winning first prize.

Did you know?
The difference between a raffle and a lottery is that lottery prizes are money, given from the money collected by selling tickets. The organizers keep the rest of the money. Raffle prizes are not money but things, which have usually been given to the organizers to help raise money for charity.

Choosing at random

If we choose something without looking, then we cannot influence the result. This means that every item is just as likely to be picked. This is called choosing at random.

Picking from a pack of cards and tossing dice are both random results where we cannot affect the result. Here is another one, when we dip into a box without looking.

The candy box

Tina had been given a present of her favorite candies in a box. On the side of the box there was a list of the contents:

> 5 toffees
> 8 soft centers
> 4 hard centers
> 7 all-chocolate

Tina prefered the soft centers. What are the chances of her getting a soft center if she just puts her hand into the box without looking?

The number of soft centers in the box is 8.

The total number of candies is:
5 + 8 + 4 + 7 = 24

So the chance of picking a soft center is:

$$\frac{\textbf{number of successes (soft centers)}}{\textbf{total number of chances (candies in the box)}} = \frac{8}{24}$$

$$= \frac{1}{3}$$

So the chances of Tina picking a soft center randomly (without looking) is **1** in **3**.

Mtoto's choice

Tina's friend Mtoto likes both toffees and all-chocolate candies. What are his chances of getting one he particularly likes?

The number of toffees and all-chocolate candies is:

5 + 7 = 12

The chances of picking either a toffee or an all-chocolate is:

$$\frac{\textbf{number of successes (toffees and all-chocolate)}}{\textbf{total number of chances (candies in the box)}} = \frac{12}{24}$$

$$= \frac{1}{2}$$

Mtoto's chances of picking what he wants is **1** in **2**, which is better than Tina because there are more candies in the box that he likes best.

Remember... Your chances of success can only be worked out if you choose randomly (without looking).

The most common – mode

In many things we do we get lots of numbers – statistics – and we often wish that we could replace them all with a single number. In these next pages you will find several important, yet simple, ideas for just that purpose. Here is the first one. It is called the "most common," or "mode."

School dinners

Peggy's class didn't think that their dinners were served fairly. When they had french fries, some of them got really big helpings, but others received less because the serving lady was in a hurry and didn't fill the scoop properly. They complained about it to their teacher. She suggested that before they complained further, they should make sure of their facts by doing a survey. The next time they had fries, everybody had to count them before they ate them and keep a note of the number. There were **30** students in the class, and they did not think that one dinner gave them enough data. So they did the survey five times, giving them:

30 × 5 = 150 results

On the right is a table, and on page 23 is a bar chart of their results.

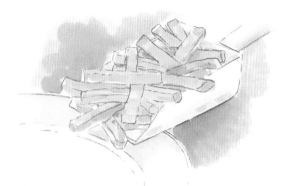

▼ **Table of the amount of fries served in each helping.**

Number of fries	Tally
15 to 19	7
20 to 24	33
25 to 29	13
30 to 34	64
35 to 39	24
40 to 45	9
Total	**150**

What was "normal"?

Look at the results. **64** people got **30** to **34** fries. This is more than any other amount. You could say that **30** to **34** was normal. This also means that those who got **15** to **19** and **20** to **24** fries had reason to feel unfairly treated.

Were there favorites?

You can also see that only **9** helpings were really big, so it wasn't true to say that it was <u>common</u> for pupils to get very large helpings.

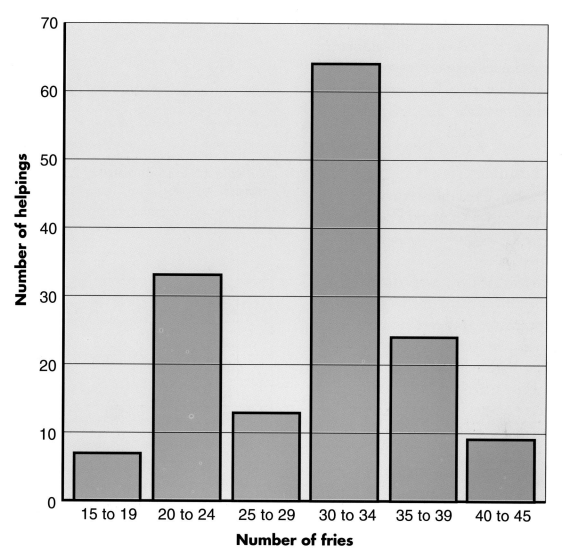

Book link... Find out more about how to make and understand charts in the book *Tables and Charts* in the *Math Matters!* set.

▼ Chart of the amount of fries served in each helping.

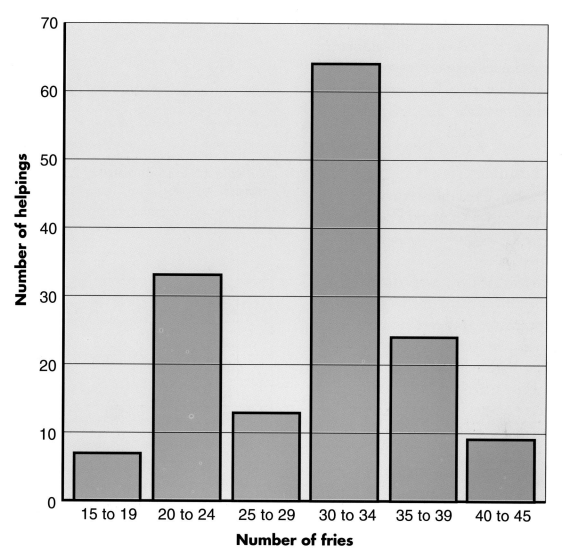

Number of helpings (y-axis: 0, 10, 20, 30, 40, 50, 60, 70)

Number of fries (x-axis: 15 to 19, 20 to 24, 25 to 29, 30 to 34, 35 to 39, 40 to 45)

What to do?

When they discussed their results, the students decided that instead of making a big fuss, next time somebody got a really small portion, they should just ask the serving lady for some more.

Remember... Mathematicians call the number or the group that occurs most often the mode. The mode is useful when you want the data to tell you what usually happens.

The middle – median

Sometimes we don't want to know which is the most common, or normal result (as we found on page 23). Instead, we might be interested in the middle value, where half the results are above and half below. Here is an example of when this is useful.

Class results

"Have you marked our tests yet, Miss Gatehouse? How did I do?"
"You got **33**, Peggy."

"Is that good?"

"It means that you were in the top half of the class, Peggy."

These are the grades that the teacher had written in her grade book for the whole class.

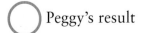
Peggy's result

Jo	**21**	Richard	**27**
Helen	**43**	Emma	**28**
Debbie	**45**	Tom	**47**
Kathy	**24**	Anne	**50**
Edwina	**47**	Najinda	**28**
Julian	**29**	Chris	**41**
Vanessa	**30**	Kevin	**42**
Amani	**45**	Elizabeth	**37**
Sebastian	**26**	Patek	**47**
Kenneth	**27**	Peter	**25**
Aziz	**47**	Damian	**27**
Jonathan	**31**	Simon	**34**
Susan	**11**	Andrew	**26**
Jennie	**23**	Peggy	**33**
Tagbo	**39**	Belinda	**47**

Here they are again, <u>arranged in order</u> in a column. Now we can easily see where Peggy came in the class. It is true that Peggy's 33 grade put her in the top half, but only just!

In this class there is not an actual middle mark because the number of pupils is even. When that happens, the middle mark is halfway between the two marks nearest the middle, in this case 31 and 33, so the middle mark is 32.

Miss Gatehouse told Peggy's parents at the parents' evening that "Peggy could have done better." When Peggy saw the marks arranged in order, she already knew that.

By the way... The mode (the mark scored most often), which gives us some idea about what is normal, is nowhere near the middle. It is 47. So it would be more normal to get 47, and using this measure, Peggy didn't do so well.

Remember... The middle mark is a useful number that mathematicians call the median. The median is useful when you want the data to tell you whether one item is in the top or bottom half of the table.

Anne	**50**	
Patek	**47**	
Belinda	**47**	
Tom	**47**	
Edwina	**47**	
Aziz	**47**	
Debbie	**45**	Top half of the class
Amani	**45**	
Helen	**43**	
Kevin	**42**	
Chris	**41**	
Tagbo	**39**	
Elizabeth	**37**	
Simon	**34**	
Peggy	**(33)**	
Jonathan	**31**	
Vanessa	**30**	
Julian	**29**	
Emma	**28**	
Najinda	**28**	
Richard	**27**	
Damian	**27**	Bottom half of the class
Kenneth	**27**	
Sebastian	**26**	
Andrew	**26**	
Peter	**25**	
Kathy	**24**	
Jennie	**23**	
Jo	**21**	
Susan	**11**	

Word check

Median: One form of average. The middle number when the data are arranged in order of size.

The average – mean

Here is the third useful way of using one value to represent many numbers. It is what people usually think of when they say average. This example shows how it works.

Hen's eggs

Peggy's grandmother kept hens. Peggy stopped in to see her after school.

"Granny, I've got to do a project on averages at school. How many eggs does a hen lay on average every week?"

"Well, let's have a look in my records."

Granny knew all her hens individually, and she had kept careful records of how many eggs each one laid for years.

Name of hen	Eggs laid in a year
Annabel	304
Beatrice	315
Clarissa	296
Dorothea	320
Eliza	312
Total eggs laid	1,547

"How can I find the average?" Peggy asked.

"Count all the eggs, and divide by the number of hens," replied Granny in a flash.

$$\text{Average} = \frac{\text{Total eggs laid}}{\text{Number of hens}}$$

"What!" exclaimed Peggy, "Why do you do it like that?"

"Because," said Granny, "when you know the average, and you go to market to buy some young hens, you can multiply the average again by the number of hens, and you will instantly know how many eggs to expect from them in a year."

"Oh!" said Peggy, "I don't think you can do that with the mode or the median."

"Of course you can't," Granny continued. "The median is the number of eggs laid in a year by the hen that falls in the middle of the order (Eliza, with 312). That's no use to me."

"The mode tells you the number of eggs most often laid. Since no two hens laid the same amount, that is not much use to me either."

"What is your kind of average called?" asked Peggy.

"Most people just call it the average," answered Granny, "but it is actually called the <u>mean</u>."

$$\textbf{Average} = \frac{\textbf{Total eggs laid (1,547)}}{\textbf{Number of hens (5)}}$$

$$= \frac{1,547}{5}$$

$$= 309.4$$

Remember... The mean is an easy form of average to work out on a calculator.

Now... Go back over the last six pages and see the different uses Peggy found for mode, median, and mean.

Word check

Average: A number that gives you, in different ways, a single typical value for the data you have. Most people use the word average when they are actually talking about the mean.

Mean: One form of average. It is calculated by dividing the total records in the data by the number of records in the data.

Book link... Find out more about dividing to get decimal numbers in the book *Decimals* in the *Math Matters!* set.

Which average should I use?

You may find it difficult to decide which of the averages to use to solve your problem. Here are some useful hints to help.

Mode: the most common value

Strengths: Simple to find from a table because it is the value that occurs most often.

Weaknesses: Only exists if there is more than one item with the same value.

When to use: Most easily used when you have a table of values that have been grouped (e.g., 1 to 5, 6 to 10, etc.), a bar chart, a pictogram, a tally chart, or a pie chart.

Median: the middle value

Strengths: Easy to find once you have a table sorted into order because it is halfway down the list.

Weaknesses: Can only be used for numbers and so cannot be found from pictograms, tallies, bar charts, or pie charts without first turning the charts into tables.

When to use: When you have a table with numbers in order, biggest at the top, smallest at the bottom or vice versa. Not worth using when you have a very big table to organize.

Mean: the total divided by the number of items

Strengths: Quick to work out using a calculator. What people first think of when you say average.

Weaknesses: Can only be used on numbers by first turning the charts into tables. The result is often not one of the values in the data.

When to use: When you have a lot of data that is not grouped or sorted into order.

Remember... First decide why you want to know an average at all. The mean is the most commonly used, so if in doubt and you have a calculator handy, use this one.

The range

Finding the average, or mean, tells us nothing about how the numbers are spread out around it. This is how to find out about the difference between the highest and lowest values, or the range. The mean usually lies in the middle of the range.

The factory visit

Miss Gatehouse took the class on a field trip to a nearby breakfast cereal factory. When they reached the machine that pours the cereal into the boxes, they found a group of managers gathered around it. Their guide explained that a new machine had just been installed, and the managers were excited because it was much more accurate than the old one.

The guide explained that if a packet labeled **500** grams contained less weight, the firm could be fined by law.

The old machine did not deliver a very precise amount of cereal. In fact, it sometimes put in as much as **520** grams or as little as **500** grams.

So the spread, or range, of amounts was **20** grams. That meant that the machine had to be set to dispense an average (mean) of **510** grams, so that the variance of **10** grams each way from the mean never fell below the minimum legal weight of **500** grams.

The new machine had a range of 4 grams, so it could be set to 502 grams, a much smaller amount over the legal amount and a great money saver.

"The managers are excited," the guide explained, "because they can save 8 grams a box on average with the new machine."

"The average here, children," interrupted Miss Gatehouse, "is the <u>mean</u>. The <u>range</u> means the difference between the smallest and the biggest of the results. It is a way of measuring <u>spread</u>, that is: how spread out the data are."

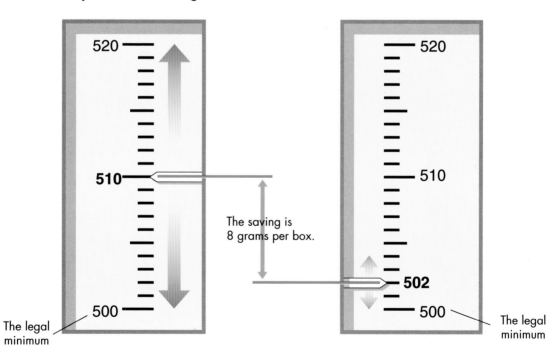

The old machine had to be set to 510 because the spread of its dispenser was so large

The new machine could be set to 502 because the spread of its dispenser was much smaller

The saving is 8 grams per box.

The legal minimum

The legal minimum

Remember... The range is useful when you want to know how spread out your results are from the mean, or average.

Word check

Range: The difference between the largest and the smallest records in data. It tells you how widely the data are spread.

Spread: A number that tells you how variable data are. It is often measured using the range.

Finding the average and range

Here is an example of how range and average could be used for a sports day.

On the School Sports Day the class was divided into five groups of six students. Each group then ran in a 100-meter race. The results of the five races are on the right with the winner (those with the quickest times) at the top of each table. The times are shown in seconds.

What is the average time taken to run the race by the winners?

To work this out, we first find the winners from the tables. Then we add up the times of the five winners:

12.6 + 12.1 + 12.0 + 13.0 + 14.1

= 63.8

And then we divide this total by 5 (the 5 winners) to get the average (mean).

$$\frac{63.8}{5} = 12.76$$

To find the average time taken by <u>all</u> the students, we need to add all the times together and divide by 30. You might want to use a calculator to do this. The total of their times is 428.7 seconds.

$$\frac{428.7}{30} = 14.29$$

Group 1	
Name	**Time**
Jo	12.6
Helen	13.1
Debbie	13.2
Kathy	13.3
Edwina	13.3
Julian	15.2

Group 2	
Vanessa	12.1
Amani	12.6
Sebastian	13.7
Kenneth	13.8
Aziz	13.8
Jonathan	15.4

Group 3	
Susan	12.0
Jennie	14.0
Tagbo	14.3
Richard	14.9
Emma	16.9
Tom	16.9

Group 4	
Anne	13.0
Najinda	13.6
Chris	13.8
Kevin	15.6
Elizabeth	15.7
Patek	16.5

Group 5	
Peter	14.1
Damian	14.3
Simon	14.6
Andrew	15.3
Peggy	15.3
Belinda	15.8

Often the most exciting race is not the fastest but the closest. So which of the races had the smallest spread of times?

We can use the range for this. We want to know which race had the smallest difference between the winner and the runner who finished last.

These are the ranges.

	Group 1	Group 2	Group 3	Group 4	Group 5
Slowest time	15.2	15.4	16.9	16.5	15.8
Fastest time	12.6	12.1	12.0	13.0	14.1
Subtract to find range	**2.6**	**3.3**	**4.9**	**3.5**	**1.7**

Group **5** was the closest race. The difference between Peter's time and Belinda's was only **1.7** seconds. This is partly because Peter was a pretty slow winner.

Remember... You can find out a number of valuable answers from one collection of results. In this case we found the mean <u>and</u> the smallest range.

Word check

Range: The difference between the largest and the smallest records in data. It tells you how widely the data are spread.

Spread: A number that tells you how variable data are. It is often measured using the range.

Using the middle and most common

In many cases the range and average can all give valuable – and different – answers. Just look at how it works in this example, which is a continuation of the story on page 33.

Sorting the argument

It was planned to have one more race between the five group winners to find the sprint champion. Jennie put her hand up to say that this was not fair. She ran faster than Peter, so why couldn't she compete instead of Peter?

By now Miss Gatehouse had entered all their times into her laptop computer, so they used the computer program to rearrange all the times in order, as shown on the right. Jennie came in 15th and Peter came in 16th.

Since there were **30** students, Jennie and Peter were in the middle. In fact, because there was an even number in the class, the middle (median) would be halfway between the two in the middle of the list. Jennie's time was **14.0**, and Peter's time was **14.1**.

The <u>median</u> was:

$$\frac{(14.0 + 14.1)}{2} = 14.05$$

Peter was not even in the top half, so Jennie had a point. But she was only one place higher. So they ran the final race between the five fastest runners instead: Susan, Vanessa, Jo, Amani, and Anne.

▼ **Sports Day 100 metre race**

Name	Time
Susan	12.0
Vanessa	12.1
Jo	12.6
Amani	12.6
Anne	13.0
Helen	13.1
Debbie	13.2
Catherine	13.3
Edwina	13.3
Najinda	13.6
Sebastian	13.7
Kenneth	13.8
Aziz	13.8
Chris	13.8
Jennie	14.0
Peter	14.1
Tagbo	14.3
Damian	14.3
Simon	14.6
Richard	14.9
Julian	15.2
Andrew	15.3
Peggy	15.3
Jonathan	15.4
Kevin	15.6
Elizabeth	15.7
Belinda	15.8
Patek	16.5
Emma	16.9
Tom	16.9
Total	428.7

The five fastest runners

The most common time (the mode)

The middle two runners (gives the median)

If we use the most common (mode), we see that the most likely time was in the top half too! Again, you can see this most easily by arranging all the times in order, as shown in the list on the left.

You can see that Kenneth, Aziz, and Chris all ran in **13.8** seconds, and no other time had as many as three hits.

The mode is more useful when the data are grouped together. If we group them in 1-second intervals, the interval from **13.0** to **13.9** seconds is the mode, with **10** hits, as shown below.

▼ **Table of results grouped into 1-second intervals**

Time (seconds)	Number of runners
12.0–12.9	4
13.0–13.9	10
14.0–14.9	6
15.0–15.9	7
16.0–16.9	3

▼ **Chart of the student times grouped into 1-second intervals**

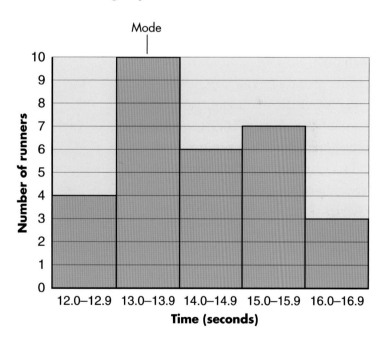

Remember... The mean, mode, and median are all different because they tell us different things about the data. Think carefully about what you want to know when deciding which to use.

Word check

Mode: One form of average. The number or the group of numbers that occurs most often in the data.

Median: One form of average. The middle number when the data are arranged in order of size.

Comparing average and range

Sometimes it is better to be brilliant and win. Sometimes it is better to be slow and steady. Here we show why this is true using average and range.

Racing rivals

Boris was a brilliant car racing driver. Some of his lap times were very, very quick. No one in the world could beat him in the right mood.

In the top chart on page 37 you can see the times it took him to go once around the track for each of **50** practice laps. The columns nearest the left are the smallest lap time, so that was when he was driving fastest.

But Boris was unreliable. In a different mood he was quite slow. His lap times have a big spread.

In the next chart you can see the practice lap times of his main rival, Darron. Can you see that Darron's three fastest laps (the column with the height **3** units on the left) were only about as fast as Boris's average?

But Darron was much more reliable. The spread of his lap times was much smaller, even though his average speed was slower.

On a good day Boris would beat Darron. But if on race day Boris was not at his best, Darron could win by being reliable.

▼ **Table of Boris's lap times**

Lap times (seconds)	Number of times
170	1
171	1
172	3
173	4
174	6
175	7
176	7
177	7
178	5
179	4
180	3
181	1
182	1
Total	50

▼ **Table of Darron's lap times**

Lap times (seconds)	Number of times
170	0
171	0
172	0
173	0
174	0
175	0
176	3
177	9
178	20
179	18
180	0
181	0
182	0
Total	50

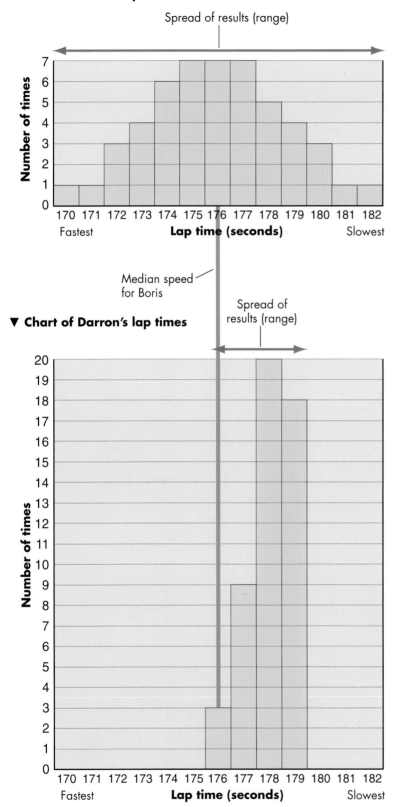

▼ **Chart of Boris's lap times**

Spread of results (range)

Number of times (y-axis: 0–7)

Lap time (seconds) (x-axis: 170–182)

Fastest — Slowest

Median speed for Boris

Spread of results (range)

▼ **Chart of Darron's lap times**

Number of times (y-axis: 0–20)

Lap time (seconds) (x-axis: 170–182)

Fastest — Slowest

What happened in the end?

Boris won the main race, scoring **10** points toward the drivers' championship for the season. Darron was second and scored **6** points. By the end of the season, though, Darron won the championship because he scored more points overall.

Remember... The most reliable racing driver was the one with the smallest range.

Good average or good spread?

Which is better, a good average or a good spread? These two examples show when it can be important to have a small spread, and when the average is unimportant.

Simon is late for school

Simon's mother took him to school by car. She was a real scatterbrain. Sometimes she got up early and missed the heavy traffic, so that Simon got to school early – too early sometimes.

Other times she got up late, stopped to buy a newspaper, was delayed in traffic, and Simon was late for school.

You can see from the top chart on page 39 that Simon was usually at school in plenty of time, but because of the large spread, about one day in ten he was late (there is a line drawn up the chart at the time when the bell rings for the start of school).

When Simon's mother could not take him, he went by bus. The small spread in the second chart shows that the bus was more reliable. When Simon went by bus, he was never late. For this reason the bus was better.

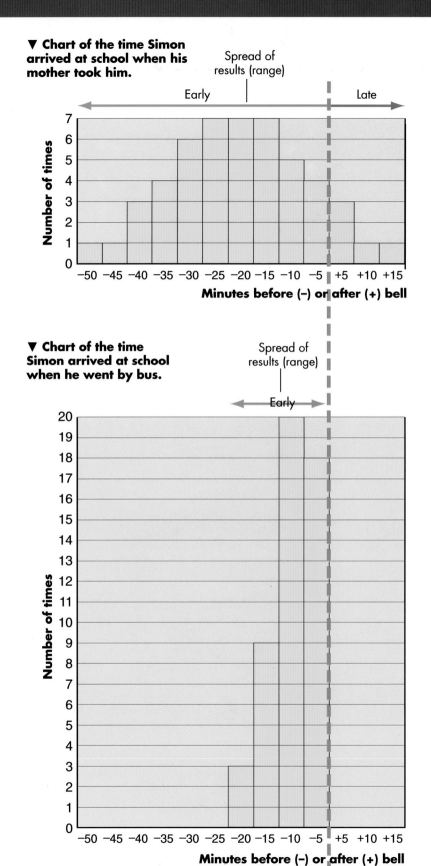

▼ **Chart of the time Simon arrived at school when his mother took him.**

Spread of results (range)

Early | Late

Number of times: 7, 6, 5, 4, 3, 2, 1, 0

−50 −45 −40 −35 −30 −25 −20 −15 −10 −5 +5 +10 +15

Minutes before (−) or after (+) bell

▼ **Chart of the time Simon arrived at school when he went by bus.**

Spread of results (range)

Early

Number of times: 20, 19, 18, 17, 16, 15, 14, 13, 12, 11, 10, 9, 8, 7, 6, 5, 4, 3, 2, 1, 0

−50 −45 −40 −35 −30 −25 −20 −15 −10 −5 +5 +10 +15

Minutes before (−) or after (+) bell

Remember… The charts on this page and on page 37 are exactly the same so that you can compare when a "good" spread is important (this page) and when a "good" average is important (page 37).

Taking samples

Suppose you want to find out how popular something is. The only real way to find out is to ask everyone. Clearly this is impossible, so mathematicians have had to think up ways of finding answers using a small number, or sample, of people. These are the rules they use.

How popular are TV programs?

TV stations need to find out how many people watch their programs. It would take too long to ask everybody. Their researchers select samples of about a thousand people, carefully chosen to match the balance of the population as a whole. They ask them what programs they watched and what they thought of them.

When the researchers have collected all the replies, they have to be sure that the answers they received are the same answers they would have got if they <u>had</u> asked the entire population.

One way to do this is to see what happens when the sample is made bigger. For example, what happens if they ask **500** people? Are the results different if they ask **1,000**, **2,000**, or **10,000** people?

Here are some answers:

People asked that day	Number who watched	percentage of viewers
40	20 out of 40	50%
100	30 out of 100	30%
500	130 out of 500	26%
1,000	240 out of 1,000	24%
2,000	480 out of 2,000	24%

In this case 1,000 people needed to be questioned before the percentage of viewers stopped changing.

Remember... The rules for samples:

1. Make sure you ask a representative group of people (for example, an equal number of young and old, women and men).

2. Keep asking more people and writing down results until the percentage doesn't change very much.

Book link... Find out about how to change fractions into percentages in the book *Fractions* in the *Math Matters!* set.

Word check
Sample: A group studied in order to find answers about a bigger group from which it has been picked.

Odds

Many people throughout the world like to place a small bet. For example, when you see horse racing on television, you will often hear people talking about odds. This is another way of talking about chance.

For example, odds of "10 to 1 against" (or just 10 to 1) means that the horse is expected to lose a race 10 times to every time it wins. So a race-goer would not be very likely to support it. Odds of 13 to 2 would be better. This means that the horse would lose 13 times for every 2 times it won, which is a ratio of only 6½ to 1.

Sometimes a horse is described as "odds-on favorite." Odds of 2 to 1 on mean that the horse is expected to win twice for every time it loses. This is a ratio of 1:2, or ½:1.

How bookmakers win on the odds

Does the odds scheme seem confusing? Bookmakers mean it to be. Bookmakers are the people who organize betting. They decide on the odds according to the amount of money they receive in bets.

Since a horse at **2** to **1** is clearly expected to win, you might think that nobody would bet on any of the others. They do so because if the one quoted at **10** to **1** actually wins, the bookmakers will pay out **10** times the money bet on it (called stake money) and return the stake money as well.

Suppose a race is run with five horses. The amount of money people bet on the horses is shown below in the table.

If Black Beauty wins at **10:1**, the bookmakers pay out **10** times the stake money in winnings to those who bet on her. **10 × 200 = 2,000**. They also return the **200** stake money, making a total payout of **2,200**. But since the bookmakers received a total in stake money on all five horses of **2,600**, they make **400** profit, because all the other gamblers lose their money.

You might like to check the arithmetic along each line for the other horses, using the same method as for Black Beauty. You will see that in each case, the bookmakers win no matter which horse wins.

Horse's name	Stake money	Secret formula	Odds to 1	Quoted odds	Prize for winners	Total payout to winners	Profit for bookmaker
My Fair Lady	1,500	0.50	0.5	2:1 ON	750	2,250	250
She's a Goer	400	4.63	4.5	9:2	1,800	2,200	300
Fancy That	300	6.50	6.5	13:2	1,950	2,250	250
Black Beauty	200	10.25	10	10:1	2,000	2,200	300
Dobbin	100	21.50	20	20:1	2,000	2,100	400

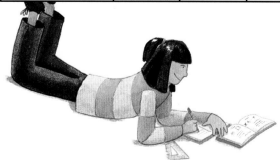

Word check

Ratio: A method of comparing different numbers by placing them on either side of a colon (:); for example, 1:2. The numbers must be measured in the same units. The order of the numbers matters. A ratio is like a fraction.

What symbols mean

Here is a list of the common math symbols together with an example of how they are used. You will find this list in each of the *Math Matters!* books, so that you can turn to any book if you want to look up the meaning of a symbol.

— Between two numbers this symbol means "subtract" or "minus." In front of one number it means the number is negative. In Latin *minus* means "less."

= The symbol for equals. We say it "equals" or "makes." It comes from a Latin word meaning "level" because weighing scales are level when the amounts on each side are equal.

+ The symbol for adding. We say it "plus." In Latin *plus* means "more."

✕ The symbol for multiplying. We say it "multiplied by" or "times."

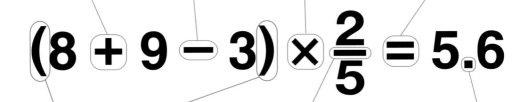

$$(8 + 9 - 3) \times \frac{2}{5} = 5.6$$

( ) Parentheses. You do everything inside the parentheses first. Parentheses always occur in pairs.

—, /, and **÷** Three symbols for dividing. We say it "divided by." A pair of numbers above and below a / or — make a fraction, so ⅖ or $\frac{2}{5}$ is the fraction two-fifths.

■ This is a decimal point. It is a dot written after the units when a number contains parts of a unit as well as whole numbers. This is the decimal number five point six or five and six-tenths.

Glossary

Other symbols in this book
% : The symbol for percent.

Terms commonly used in this book.

Average: A number that gives you, in different ways, a single typical value for the data you have. Most people use the word average when they are actually talking about the mean.

Bias: A fair test can be upset when there is not an equal chance of something happening. This effect is called bias.

Chance: Something that occurs in an unpredictable way. You can forecast your chances in the long term, but you can never guarantee what will happen next.

Choices: The things we actually pick from what is available.

Data: Information from which you start to solve a problem. You might have collected it yourself or have been given it. The word comes from Latin meaning "things given."

Decimal number: A number that contains parts of units as well as whole units. The decimal point is used to separate the units from the parts of a unit.

Equally likely: Results are called equally likely when there is no reason to think any one of them will occur more often than the others. In an experiment they still might not occur the same number of times. That's chance!

Even: An equal chance of achieving one of the two possible results, such as in coin tossing.

Fraction: A special form of division using a numerator and denominator. The line between the two is called a dividing line.

Lottery: A game of chance in which tickets are sold, and the prizes are in the form of money

Mean: One form of average. It is calculated by dividing the total records in the data by the number of records in the data. *See* Median and Mode.

Median: One form of average. The middle number when the data are arranged in order of size. *See* Mean and Mode.

Mode: One form of average. The number or the group of numbers that occurs most often in the data. *See* Mean and Median.

Options: The set of equally likely things we can pick from.

Percent: A number followed by the % symbol means the number is divided by 100. It is a way of writing a fraction.

Raffle: A fund-raising lottery with goods as prizes.

Range: The difference between the largest and the smallest records in data. It tells you how widely the data are spread. *See* Spread.

Ratio: A method of comparing different numbers by placing them on either side of a colon (:); for example, 1:2. The numbers must be measured in the same units. The order of the numbers matters. A ratio is like a fraction.

Sample: A group studied in order to find answers about a bigger group from which it has been picked.

Sector: A piece of a circle, like a piece of a pie.

Spread: A number that tells you how variable data are. It is often measured using the range. *See* Range.

Set index